Erik,

You have always had wisdom and soulfulness far deeper than your years. I hear you speak on things with an understanding and conviction that takes most people far longer to understand. Personally, I often wonder where and how you came by such a fully realized awareness of ambition, integrity and purpose.
Bottom line, we love you and your wife and look forward to all that is to come your way.

With Thanks and Fondness,

Shauna and Greg Pinneo

Perhaps one of the greatest testimonials we ever received is a testament to our real estate credibility to perform. As you will read about in this book, we received a lead from a mail man that led to us purchasing this families whole portfolio over several years.
This was their testament to doing business with us.

> Karen,
>
> Again, a big thank you to you, Eric + your team of professionals for a yet another hassle free property sale.
>
> Due to your dilligence, I am now a RETIRED LANDLORD!!
>
> Best of luck in your ventures,
> David Kellogg
> + Mom!!

Read What Others Are Saying About Erik Stark

Good Morning Erik, First off, let me say that Erik Stark continues to give away free GOLD and this book is no different. However, and before I say, "what gives?!?" to you for imparting tons and tons of competition — possibly — in my direct farm area, let me say with a sigh of relief, that the gift of this particular conversation will go UNUSED by 99.999% of all investor/ listeners/readers. Why? Because it implies that one will actually have to WORK for one's leads and make GENUINE, PERSONAL CONNECTIONS with one's lenders/buyers/sellers. Since Erik helped shift our business from impersonal, computer-based lead "wishing," in essence,... to active, face-to-face and genuine lead CREATION, my phone has started ringing, my email account is filling, and my appointment calendar is filling. Period.

Your Friend
Mark Kramer

I've watched Erik & Steve grow from front row seminar attendees to special guest panelists at our events sharing the stage with us guru's. They are living testimony of outstanding real estate success and they actively crush their market every day in their business. I love these guy's and you should listen to them!

Than Merrill-Founder of Fortune Builders

Good Morning Erik,

I just wanted to thank you for all of the knowledge and motivation you have shared with me. Between our Phone Calls, Text Messages and your Instagram posts you have been a wealth of information and I wouldn't have closed my first assignment deal for 5k without you. God bless 🙏

Carlos Coppins Jr.

How To Buy Your First Real Estate Property
(and Your Next 100)

An Uncommon Approach to Finding Off Market, Competition Free Properties in Any Market

Erik Stark
Marketer, Investor, Husband, Dad

A Publication of TheRealErikStark.com

Copyright 2018 Erik Stark

All Rights Reserved. No part of this book may be used, reproduced or transmitted in any manner, mechanical or electronic whatsoever without prior written consent from the author.

This publication is designed to provide accurate and authoritative information with regard to the subject matter covered. By no means is this giving professional, legal or investing advice and should you consider investing you should consult your legal professional about the risks involved. The information shared has been the authors experience and far from typical results.

The notes, ideas, case studies and results in this book are real life scenarios. One should not consider these results as typical.

The forms used in this book are actual documents used by our firm. One should not consider any real estate document to be a one size fits all application. Different states and municipalities have their own legal requirements. Therefore you should seek the guidance of a competent attorney or CPA before using any documents and investing.

Dedication's

This book is dedicated to God almighty, who gave me these incredible abilities and the heart to share them with the world.

To my wife, Michelle who shined her brightest when the accounts were low and the situation seemed bleak. You always believed.

To our son, Kaiden who keeps my Why ever so clear and gives life to my days.

To my partner, Steve who is one of my greatest personal mentors in life and was there before any of this was even a vision in our minds.

To my parents, Mike and Michelle, Thank you for always believing in me and never shutting down my insatiable desire to always have another goal to live up to. You felt my pain and supported my struggle.

Most importantly, this book is dedicated to you, the reader, who seeks the diligent path to fruition. It is my wish that you use this book and the knowledge imparted on you to go farther than you ever dreamed. I know real estate can get you there.

Dare to let your mind wander into greatness.

You are so much stronger than you give yourself credit for.

I believe in you.

Table of Contents

Introduction:..11

Chapter 1: Identifying Your Farm Area...............18

Chapter 2: Generating Leads...............................33

Chapter 3: How Many Leads/Appointments Did You Get /Go On This Week?..64

Chapter 4: Making Intelligent Offers...That Stick 75

Chapter 5: Closing The Deal………………..…..86

Chapter 6: Building Relationships With Buyers Who Know Like and Trust You to Buy From You? ……………………………………………………100

Chapter 7: Growing and Scaling Your Real Estate Business...110

Chapter 8: Bonus Chapter The Real Secret Behind Success...129

Conclusion: What It Takes To Buy Property!....138

Free Resources and Appendix........................140

"As to methods there may be a million and then some, but principles are few. The man who grasps principles can successfully select his own methods. The man who tries methods, ignoring principles, is sure to have trouble."

Emerson

>   "Everything Popular is Wrong"
>   -Oscar Wilde

Introduction

I want to first off thank you for your time you are investing in yourself. I take it upon myself with great responsibility that you chose to spend your time with me, and therefore promise to be a good steward of the time you have allotted us to spend together.

I would also like apologize for a little brutal truth I am about to share with you. This book you are holding was created for two reasons.

1. If you're able, you're obligated. So it is my duty to teach what I have been blessed with.
2. Perhaps my results alone don't qualify me as an educator, however, the biggest paydays I have ever received were those when others cracked the code and changed their lives through real estate.

I digress.

I remember the days of my first deal (I still keep the check stub in my binder as a reminder).

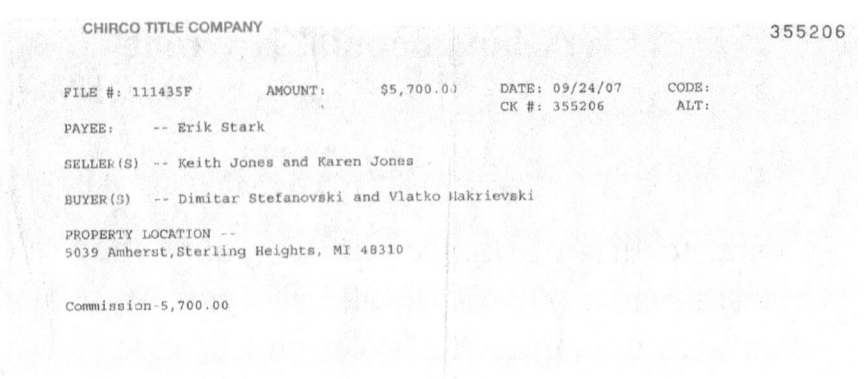

...just know that I can relate to your situation.

I have been exactly where you are right now.

We don't have time for that right now, yet before you read further, why you should even listen to a word I say?

Who the heck is Erik Stark anyway?

Consider that I have spent over $250,000 on my real estate education. Have done well over 400 real estate deals (residential, multi unit, commercial, new construction, land developments, estates, REO, private owner, FSBO, retiring landlords, family portfolios, etc).

I have coached for educators such as Greg Pinneo at his Power Players Intensive, Than Merrill for the Fortune Builders Mastery Program, Preston Ely and the REO Rockstar Program, have been the BETA tester for products such as Freedomsoft, Realeflow, Fortune Builders Mastery, Wholesaling U and spent my own personal 10,000+ hours in the field of real estate, acquisition, finance, negotiation and business development. I've seen it, done it, tested it, verified what works and built a repeatable algorithm based on those results.

More important than anything, I have made mistakes. A ton of them. I still do. Mistakes that cost me tens of thousands of dollars, agony over my decision and responsibility to correct it. I see too many people who stand on stage and tell how they repeatedly win over and over again. If you're not failing, I cannot relate to you or you are just moving way to slow in life.

"If You Have Everything Under Control, You Are Not Moving Fast Enough"
                                           Mario Andretti

I need to drive these principles into your head hard and fast. While every entrepreneur wants to have a nice primary castle for his family, a fleet of Italian steeds outside and access to a private jet, the real reason we get into real estate is **freedom.**

What does any of those items have to do with real estate anyway?

They SELL people on the dream. The dream of high income is what attracts people to real estate. **Just so we are clear, its FREEDOM we are all after.**

Money is just the tool.

Many people get into real estate with dreams of making high income.

Then they begin making high income and realize they are trading many, long hours for that high income. Thats not what FREEDOM is about. However, we will teach you more about freedom and automation down the road.

Right now, we are here to show you how to buy your first real estate property. Before we begin digging deep, know that there will be MANY distractions to steer you away from your path to greatness. Put on your blinders to much of what you see. Don't abandon your goal because you see someone else making money over there. Principles of real estate will never change. Know that. The form in which they are pitched to you change daily. Know that too.

Doing your first deal is an incredible breakthrough. Your brain salivates just in seeing a lead become a deal, to an agreement, to a valuable asset in the eyes of the buyer, to an exchange of property for money and at the end everyone is satisfied and you just made a handsome profit leveraging the horsepower of real estate. You likely didn't even recognize that I just explained how to flip a house.

Thats just ONE of the many ways to do it.

My first deal I gave away 60% of my profit to get the deal done. I would do it again just to be able to sit in front of a check with my name that was equal to two months pay from my previous J.O.B (just over broke).

Listen, I'm not a very brilliant person. For what I lack in smarts, I likely make up in work ethic. However, I am living breathing proof that a car flipping, auto detailer with no bloodline of family entrepreneurs, armed only with a deeply rooted desire to make something of myself so I could provide for my wife and our newborn son, can make real estate his full time income, giving me control over my time so I can be there for my family.

If I can make that a reality, I am placing my bets that there are other driven souls that just want to do, have and be more in life than what was dealt to them.

I am making my bet that you can do this do. With resources like this book, the Real Estate While You Drive podcast and constant access to my team and I via social media, there is no way you cannot make it.

Invest in yourself. Take your education serious. Commit to **massive action** and build a unique process for keeping motivated when thoughts grow weary.

I believe in you. We are in this walk together.

CHAPTER

1

Define Your Farm Area!

What is a farm area?

Your farm area is the land that you are going to know everything about.

The sales statistics.

Price per sq. ft.

The boundaries.

Which subdivisions are better?

Mary who is always out pruning her garden and knows what is going on in this neighborhood more than any Realtor cause she has lived here for three decades.

Who's buying.

What agent controls the market place.

How many listings are currently active?

Who the city inspector is for that neighborhood?

The list of properties he is tired of violating each month.

And the address of every distressed and desirable property in that area.

Your farm area is the area that you are going to master.

It is crucial to start off in one area and master that area. Find out where all the sales activity is in your local area and make that your farm area. The problem with starting off fresh and chasing deals all over town is you never master anything. You end up scrambling, getting frustrated and putting your dream on the back shelf. If you REALLY want to excel in real estate, you must **learn work a strategy, and not chase opportunity.**

FIND YOUR FARM AREA AND MASTER IT.

The term *farm area* has been a part of real estate since before you and I joined the industry. If you relate to a real farm, a farmer knows his land. EVERY bit of it.

You MUST do the same with your territory. The more time you spend walking the land, the more you will harvest. **Do not forget that metaphor.** Walk the land and plant seeds every where you go.

There is no harvest without seeds.

Let me tell you about one of our most profitable farm areas.

It's a working class neighborhood with above average incomes. The properties have classic brick character and the downtown has an incredible pulse for entrepreneurs and business owners, as well as those who venture to this town to enjoy its cafes, art, unbiased conversations about life and incredible dining experiences.

Within this one market, we have done large assignment deals, major rehabs, purchased performing rentals, built new homes, done large developments and purchased a portfolio of properties from one family.

This is in an area of less than 4 square miles with less than 20,000 residents.

We specialize in this farm area.

Yet we continuously mail and stir up opportunities in this one area. We drive these streets often to find new opportunities. Whenever we buy a new property here, we mail the neighborhood and have them come see what we are doing to improve the value of their homes (who doesn't like that).

When we sell a property and are looking for a replacement, we mail the neighborhood and let them know.

When we have an open house coming up, we let the immediate neighbors know that they can choose their own neighbor by bringing a buyer.

Simple ways to add value without pestering your audience.

We could spread ourselves throughout several counties and **_possibly_** do more deals, however, we run a tight ship in this little farm area and it seems to be rewarding us well, especially as we gain more market share each passing year.

Working a strategy in a few solid farm areas like this makes for a rewarding life, business and future wealth building.

I recommend finding a farm area close to your home. You do not want to spend a lot of time driving **to** your area each day. You want to **spend time IN your farm area each day**. Later on we will learn how to expand our areas, for now, lets master the territory.

You can google the terms "heat maps" or "sales statistics" for your local county or city and **find out where investors and buyers are buying *the most property***. This is where you want to saturate yourself in. Do not worry about the competition. Most of them are lazy, computer screen investors and those who do not spend time in the streets lose the most opportunity.

Here are a few free tools to help you with finding your farm area.

https://www.trulia.com/home_prices/

https://www.nar.realtor/research-and-statistics/housing-statistics

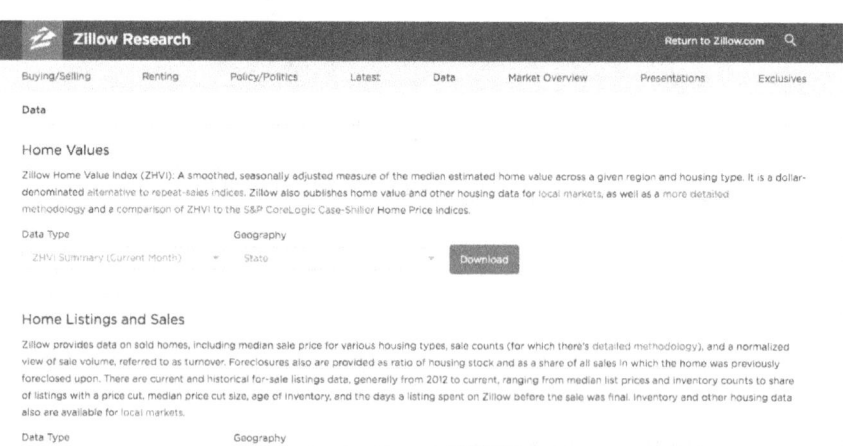

https://www.zillow.com/research/data/

www.housingalerts.com

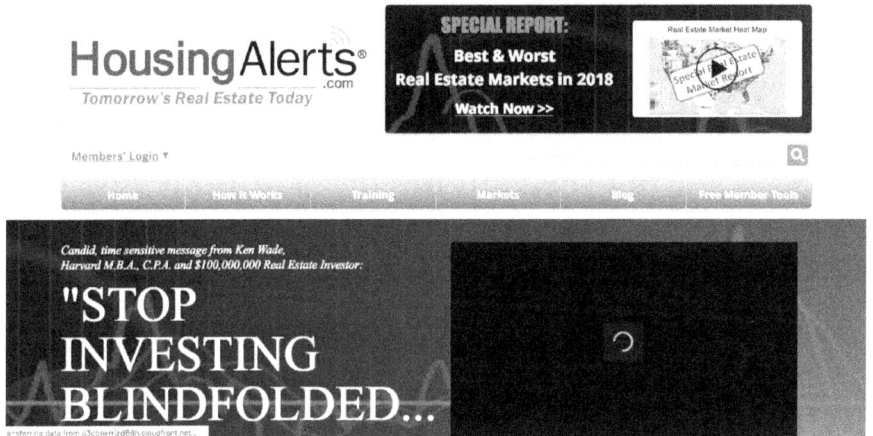

Google "Your City Here" GIS Maps

Use these tools to your advantage. Take this information serious and you can make serious money.

I tend to spend a good amount of time in the streets. We have made a small fortune flipping houses by being active every day in our farm area.

Sure we have flipped homes from the beach or on vacation but that would have never happened if we did not put the seeds in the ground to harvest later on.

A computer can only offer so much.

When you drive/walk/ride the streets you are able to be in depth with the marketplace. What areas sell faster? Why? Who's buying? For how much?

We'll get into running virtual business models later, for now, these are crucial factors to master.

While you're driving, keep a yellow pad of paper with you. Write down the address and some notes to research when you get home.

(Side Note: I actually keep several yellow pads when I drive through my farm areas. I organize my yellow pads so I have one just for distressed sellers, one for buyers I see rehabbing, one for buyers I see building houses, and then I even find out who is lending on those houses just bought. Lastly, I keep a yellow pad for the absolute classic, gorgeous in demand properties we want to own. These become what we call our Top 100. The ones that change the game. As you will see if you are diligent, these yellow pads come to life. Nowadays you can also use smartphone apps such as https://www.godrivingfordollars.com/. This app will generate a route, show your areas you have already driven, show you where the distressed properties you marked

are on the map, research the owners and place them into a database so you can begin mailing them right away.)

Im old school and have yellow pads all over the place, so naturally, I use yellow pads, even with todays new and easy technology.

I digress.

Others you may choose to leave a note behind informing them of your interest.

I do both.

Leave a oversized sticky note AND mail them. We'll talk more of that in the next chapter.

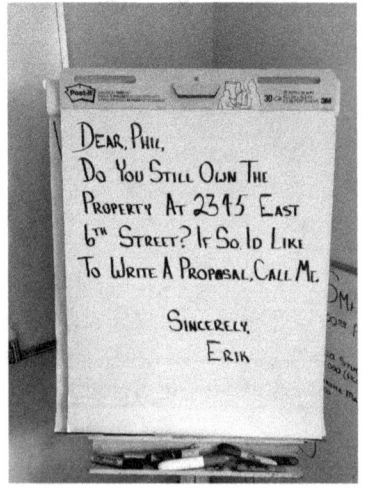

The goal I want you to understand is that your name needs to be so well known in that area, when someone sneezes real estate, the neighbor brings a tissue box over with your name on it. **If you don't have a lot of money, you will use your time** to find this info and build your name. Flyers, postcards and door hangers are all proven marketing pieces that get your phone to ring. Even more so is true about a handwritten note.

We'll talk about more of this in the next chapter, however, get in the habit of leaving notes, dropping postcards, having conversations about opportunities. The more places your message and services can be found, you'll largely increase your chances of capitalizing on those opportunities.

Bottom line, find your farm area and prepare to secretly dominate a select few, off market properties you can take down and sell (or keep) for huge financial benefit.

Do you have a market in mind?

Lets proceed.

Action Steps from Chapter 1

Determine your ideal farm area.

Use the tools above to find areas with high sales activity.

Make sure its close to your home so you can quickly spend time on your farm, planting seeds of opportunity.

Download the Go Driving For Dollars App to your smart phone and create an account to begin collecting addresses.

Buy some yellow pads for jotting down addresses and leaving notes behind.

Print out a map of your farm area. We prefer zoning maps, which show you different zoning areas around the city.

(Side Note - Understanding zoning can take the average profit of a deal and supercharge it. Many old homes that were built under old zoning codes are now zoned with greater density and worth WAY more to the developer market. Begin to learn zoning. It pays in the future. Maybe the immediate future!)

CHAPTER

2

How To Generate Leads

Now that you have your farm area picked out, you need to begin planting seeds in the ground.

Seeds are the marketing pieces and conversations you will have that will reap a harvest.

There are two main ways to generate leads.

Marketing vs. Prospecting

Marketing — *Direct Prospecting*

"Many people think of prospecting and marketing as mutually exclusive, but I encourage you to think bigger and see them as *mutually supportive*. Your prospecting can be supported or enhanced by your marketing and your marketing can be supported or enhanced by your prospecting."

—Gary Keller, Keller Williams Realty,
Author of *The Millionaire Real Estate Agent*

Prospecting and Marketing. We're going to teach you how to blend them both.

Knocking on someones door to ask if they will sell you their house is prospecting. This is an active approach to investing and generally requires you to qualify them for needing your services. A great way to generate leads.

Mailing someone and asking if they will sell you their house is marketing. This is a passive approach and allows you to simply discover who is in need of your services. Another great way (actually greater since you wont deal with the rejections common with prospecting) to generate leads.

Lead generation and marketing became my most passionate part of real estate because **in order to get good harvest, you must have superior seeds.**

I've become obsessed with finding out WHY the 15% of buyers act immediately and why the remaining 85% still needed time before they took action.

What is the "salt" we use to lead that horse to water to get a drink?

Pushing someone to take action rarely ever works.

Educating them with all their options so they can make an honest decision and take action when they are ready works every time.

There are multiple ways to plant seeds in your farm. Putting postcards, door hangers, handwritten notes or even a sticky note on the front door of EVERY distressed home you see while out in the field is a great way.

The reason is because so few people spend time in their field so they are not reaching these people in the same way you can.

They depend on a list and a mailed postcard to get a response (which is what so many people do). For some investors, it works well. For most, their postcard gets lost in the "shuffle".

We just prefer a different, more focused approach to direct mail. A handwritten note taped on the front door is a great way to have a different approach.

Sellers typically sell when they are motivated.

Distressed property owners are far more motivated to sell than dolled up, financially fit property owners. You cannot identify distressed properties unless your are in the streets laying your eyes on it.

Even though list providers have tried to create filters that can determine if someone is leading down the path of physical distress, the only sure fire way is to lay your eyes on it.

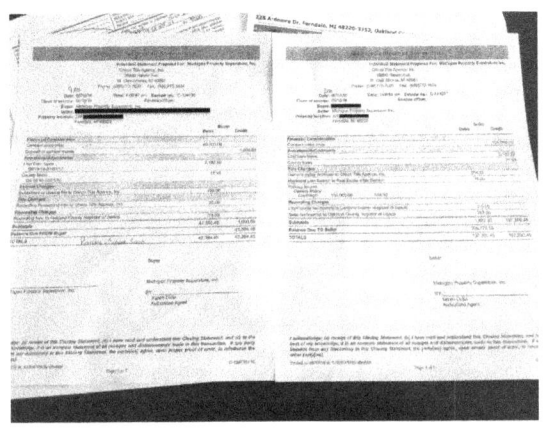

I have been a big fan of making big money from small lists for the last several years. Lists that were mostly hand picked and cannot be purchased online. This was a $64,000 profit from a $40,000 purchase that came from that hand picked list.

Knowing the response statistics of direct mail, I knew we could increase our responses by removing the majority of the **unqualified** recipients from a mailing campaign and focusing on those most probable.

By doing this, we are able to mail specifically to a 100% qualified list of verifiable property situations and characteristics and then reach out to them to discover who is interested in what we have to offer.

This is also the perfect time to begin crafting your perfect message. Although I often think along the lines of direct response marketing messages, I tend to blend that scientific approach to advertising with a dash of authentic, genuine interest in buying their property.

Lets look at a few marketing messages and let me know which you would respond to or at minimum, notice there is a big difference in who you may choose to do business with.

"Cash For Your Home In 3 Days. No Repairs. No Commissions"

or

"Sell Your Property For Top Dollar, In The Shortest Time, With The Least Amount of Hassle"

Different people would analyze this in multiple different ways, however, lets just look at it from a seller benefit standpoint.

Cash for your home in 3 days sounds ok. However, that doesn't mean it's a lot of cash. It has been our experience that the savvy property owners consider those cash in a flash guys, exactly that. Quick turn, fly by night, low ball cash offer guys with no real basis of accurate business acumen. This may not be 100% true, its just a common comment we heard when trying to apply the "fast cash" message to higher end properties.

Now, what if you were to consider selling for top dollar in the shortest time with the least amount of hassle?

This doesn't necessarily mean you're getting top dollar in cash. However the benefits are clear.

Top Dollar (which honestly is the fair market value of a property aka what buyer and seller agree upon)

Shortest time (everyone loves speediness)

Least amount of hassle (we are not there to finagle with the seller and beat up the price. The goal is a fair deal for their property).

Years ago, we began collecting mailers from other investors, so we knew what messages were being sent out to the market. We chose a direct opposite of approach from the masses.

You can find a few sample letters and postcards on the resources page at http://therealerikstark.com/resources/.

Again, these are the mailers from other investors, not our own. We have a private library of proven messages and drip campaigns available to students of our mastermind group. These messages offer totally different Unique Seller Propositions and change the dynamic of our positioning in the marketplace. Like the one you read above.

Over the years, I have repeatedly heard that the reason they called us is because our letter was very genuine and sincere.

The second reason is that when they went through their file, they had more mailers from us than any other investor.

It's no secret in marketing that he who can pay the most for a lead, wins. Real estate is a big ticket business and there are big ticket expenses.

However, there are several ways to get leads, that cost very little money and only require your time.

We look forward to getting you to the point where you have more money to pay for leads, but for getting you to buy your first deal, there are some great low cost ways to stir up opportunity. The best part about these leads, is you are building a list of absolutely qualified property owners who all have the right criteria for you to begin having a conversation.

Before we begin getting into the lead flow portion of this chapter, I want to help you discover some options for capturing your leads.

I prefer to answer most of my calls live. Now keep in mind, these are very focused mailers, to mid to high end neighborhoods, including multi family properties, apartments and commercial.

So I know each time my money line rings we have just "discovered" a new customer who wants our services. Much of our qualifying has already been done.

That phone call is basically lining us up for a face to face meeting, with much of the heavy lifting already out of the way because they have several ways to get educated about how we help.

Depending on what campaign they called from, we know that they are already sold on the fact that we are showing up to pay cash at a below market price.

Or they may be wanting to sell their property and continue to receive an income, therefore they have been educated about our SmartSell System.

These calls are not the typical name, rank serial number like most pre screening calls investors do.

Back to business.

However, I am also a big fan of helping new investors set themselves up for success.

So lets talk lead capture systems for a moment.

Google Voice offers a free solution to your phone system situation. With a simple G-Mail account, you can choose a custom number (keep in mind that response rates increase when you have the same area code as the people you are mailing).

You can set this up to ring right to your phone, or pre screen them through a pre recorded message or you can get really fancy and screen the listeners as they are talking and pick up once you know they are ready to have a serious discussion.

The great thing about Google Voice is you can use the recording as a pre recorded message to further qualify prospects before you speak to them. You can also forward all calls to an assistant, transcribe through email and text. It also serves as a storage database of all your callers.

For a free service, this is a great way to get set up.

If you don't mind spending $12 per month, you can set up a true prerecorded message service and have all the functionality of a professional company through ITeleCenters message service.

Having a pre recorded message is a great way to increase call volume. Often times, many people want to take action but don't in fear of having to expose something painful about life or the property to a real person.

By giving them the option to call a pre recorded line to find out more, this removes the pressure they feel they would have to face if someone were to pick up the phone.

I also recommend a very simple, non invasive website to capture your leads. I'll be honest, we rarely receive a website lead that stemmed from a direct mail response. Most savvy sellers are willing to pick up the phone and get right to the matter at hand and don't need to dance around anything.

However, websites are so cheap nowadays and you can surely pick up some good leads by having a website for capturing leads.

Companies like www.RealeFlow.com have very low cost, simple plug and play websites you can have set up and fully optimized in less than a days time.

We give people the option to contact us in multiple ways. Website for more info, prerecorded line, email, text and live answer.

You can bank on the masses of onesie, twosie property owners to find out more about what you do without having to fully immerse themselves in your world.

However, higher end property owners and professional landlords will likely just pick up the phone and get right to business.

For a true bootstrap operation, you can use a telephone, a yellow pad, some envelopes, stamps and a cell phone. This podcast will tell you How To Start Real Estate For Less Than $100

If we are considering having a life of freedom and enjoying the money we will be earning, we want to implement these paid systems to take the load off of you having to be available all the time.

Now that we have discussed a little about phones and websites, lets get back into generating leads.

Here are the best ways to begin getting leads from your farm area. I break this down in two ways.

Those that are low cost and those that cost money.

Keep in mind, the goal is not to never spend money. If you are just beginning, this will get you going.

However, once you begin cashing checks, it would be wise to use some of those proceeds to purchase systems, leads and team members to truly help you grow a business.

Low Cost Lead Sources Are:

Driving for Dollars and Collecting the Addresses of Distressed Property and Beautiful Properties - *Tried and true method many veterans swear by.*

Talking With Neighbors About Vacant Properties, Problem Properties and Potential Up and Coming Opportunities

Talking to Mail Men (YES this works. *We bought a portfolio of properties from one family from a mailman lead)*

Hunting Deals on Craigslist, Zillow and Trulia and Calling the Owners of Properties for Rent (*Tasks like this are perfect for a $3/hour virtual assistant. More on that later)*

Getting Probate Leads and Mailing Them Weekly (We LOVE Probates)! These are great for many reasons. <u>**Small focused lists allow you to keep the cost down and also create very consistent, personal, focused mailers.**</u>

Probates have BY FAR been very profitable deals over our career. The lists are small each week and you can create a great campaign around providing value to these situations.

Internet Commercials (iMercials) with keyword rich content *(with social media being a source of free traffic, get in the habit of putting your messages out to your audience, use the power of video to record successful closings where you can showcase the property owners own words about doing business from you).*

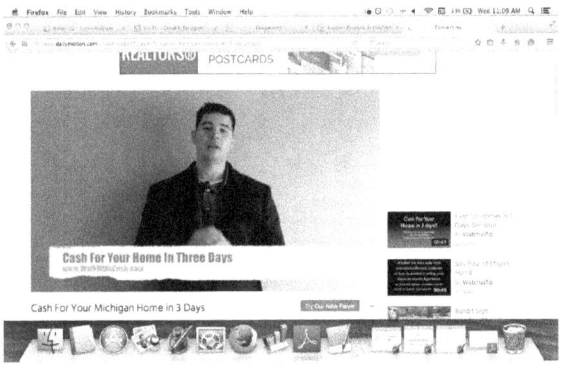

Leads from Realtors. *Look, agents get paid when they perform. Most agents aren't going to drop their niche to only work on your model, however, getting to know the agent who does a lot of probates is a good agent to know. Getting in touch with an agent who lists divorce sale properties or distressed homes is a good relationship to cultivate. We have case studies stacked where agents delivered us deals that we very well knew the market would have paid more on. It works. And its free.*

I assure you that if you take this seriously and approach this with tenacity, you will literally watch your activity escalate each week.

A conversation here returns a call here.

A note left behind generates an appointment.

Again, there will be many ways we will teach you to find leads. These are quick, affordable ways to get you to buy your first real estate property.

We also still buy a property or two per year just from keyword searches we use to search craigslist. Words like motivated seller, owner finance, investment, land contract, original owner, needs tlc, handyman, investor. These same key words apply to MLS searches if you have access.

Moving on.

High Cost Lead Sources:

Direct Mail Campaigns (Mailing 10s of thousands of mailers each week). *We did this our first year into doing direct mail and I became frustrated at the amount of unqualified leads we were mailing and calls we were receiving. I know many investors who do really well with this and make big money, however I prefer to make big money with small mailing lists.*

Online Pay Per Click Advertising (Google, Facebook). *This is becoming ever more popular in real estate. However, much of our target market is not online so we do not focus in this area.*

Bus Benches These work well when you have a series of benches or billboards. However, don't think one month on one bench will have a huge impact.

Newspaper Ads (Classified ads are still affordable, however, if you want to stick out, we recommend 1/4 to 1/2 page advertorial ads.) Advertorials are great because they do not come across as sales copy, but rather useful information.

Radio Advertising Radio ads can be really good if positioned properly. Many times, as humans, we put a lot of trust in our local radio show hosts and if we are able to genuinely and authentically educate those radio shows about how we really help people, they can earn the loyalty of their audience to do business with you. However, much of todays radio ads are shameless plugs of paid advertising with no real substance to the ad. Get to know your local radio and tv shows. Support them in their events and before long, they may personally want your services and then, they become a walking advocate for your excellence.

Many paid advertising forms are created for long term branding purposes. Branding is tough and can be very expensive.

As where, direct response can create an ad on Monday, run the ad on Tuesday and usually pay for the advertisement cost by the time the invoice arrives because it generates an immediate response.

The difference in cost for these situations is that it's not expensive to run one radio ad, or a newspaper ad.

However the goal is to be consistent so you want to plan to run your campaign a few months out.

For example, if you are going to begin doing newspaper advertising, you don't want to spend your whole budget on putting your ad in every newspaper just for this week.

We have had great success, by NOT putting it in every newspaper and going right back to our farm area and running an ad for 6 months in that paper only.

Now we are hyper focused on the target market, are planning to be visible longer and have a true budget laid out for consistent marketing.

So the big expense is not in this weeks ad, but in running the ad consistently for months or years.

Let me help by reframing this thought in your brain.

All marketing is a test. We have ran some tests that were complete failures and still made us $15,000. Others, we thought were so perfect that we were going to get flooded and received very little.

None of those "tests" were an expense. They were an investment in our business.

You do have to be mindful as you can create so much of an "investment" that the leads never convert to deals fast enough and you spend more than you make.

Then when you quit, it becomes an expense because you are no longer investing money to get a return. **If you don't know how to create unique marketing pieces with great offers and response mechanisms and how to track response rates, this is worth getting educated as it can easily cost more than its worth.**

It is also worth mentioning that **placing ads specific to your target audiences demographics, is a prime factor in marketing success.**

Many of our target property owners are over the age of 50 and many of them are not on Facebook. Therefore a Facebook ad wouldn't do us any good.

We do however get great responses from print advertising, flyers, newspaper ads, diner placemats and advertorials. That is where the majority of our markets eyes are focused.

This is one of the pillars we teach at our marketing workshops and masterminds is to build your specific avatar for each market you market to.

This report may help you narrow down your target market

If you miss this one step, you'll miss the majority of your audience.

Back to Buying Your First Real Estate Property.

At all times we are typically doing 4-9 different lead generators and those include direct mail, networking, a LOT of street driving and talking with neighbors and owners, sifting craigslist, newspaper ads and calling a lot of Realtors.

One of my absolute best sources for leads came from a pissed off seller who called me and left me a nasty message not to ever call her or mail her again. She was PISSED. So I did what most will not do and picked up my phone and called her back.

I made that lady my friend that day.

Turned out her and her husband owned a very nice portfolio of properties. My partner and I bought most of them. They lent us over $250,000 at 5% interest and most importantly, he introduced me to ALL the old school landlords from the Rotary Clubs, Optimist Clubs and around town. He took a liking to us so much that he told all his friends, when you are ready to sell, sell to "my guys" right here. **It is a slower game but when you get a lead from guys like him, you walk right into that appointment with so much horsepower** behind you that **no other investor stands a chance**. Once you are in, you are IN.

To me, that is a secret faucet. Not a magic one, but a secret one. No one talks about it because it isn't sexy, but it has allowed us to put a unique stranglehold on a portion of the market that no one else will have access to.

The purpose I told you that story is for you to understand what is possible when you go against the rut of conformity.

I could have just removed her like she asked.

That call could have really blown up in my face.

However, I sincerely felt she was making a judgement on us based on what she was feeling about the majority of our industry.

I know deep down that we are not the majority and that I only had a few seconds to make that statement stick in her mind.

This time it worked in our favor. Sometimes it doesn't. However, you can increase those actions that wind up in your favor by making it common practice to do what others wont.

*What we really want is the relationship. **<u>THAT</u>** is what gets deals done.*

So here is what you need to do.

<u>If you have the money,</u> determine whether you will send post cards or letters. Postcards usually work better in lower end markets. Higher end property owners are savvy and the way to their hearts is sincerity and authenticity. You can buy lists such as probates, absentee owners, bankruptcy, foreclosure defaults and many others and begin mailing them. This is a deep rabbit hole and I cannot stress enough how important it is to have effective marketing.

I can also help with this.

Direct mail is the greatest way to get leads from my experience. Just know it costs money and you will want to track the expenses, amount of mailers, responses, which lists respond best, which mailers gets the most responses. This testing can rarely be avoided while you build a repeatable algorithm.

In marketing and in life, you are either consistent or non existent.

Your marketing MUST differ from the competition or you just blend in.

Side Note: I encourage you to educate your audience instead of badgering them. If possible, find someone who owns a lot of property to start collecting the mailers they get and create something totally opposite. Looking at all 10+ mailers from local competition, will show you EXACTLY what NOT TO DO. You should stop and imagine just how powerful this strategy is. Imagine having ALL of your competitors mail pieces.

If you want to master probates, create a unique process to educate people going through the probate process on "7 Must Know Facts About Selling A Property in Probate".

Then you follow up with a document checklist.

Then you explain to them how to file paperwork in that county.

Then you offer a list of the 5 best attorneys for handling probates.

Then you have a list estate sale companies to help them clear out the contents.

These companies should have some strategic alliance with you so they can refer your services to them when it comes time to sell. It is your duty to align these relationships.

Sure it may seem overwhelming, however it can be created one time and then it works like a 24 hour slave for your business, always generating new prospects into your world.

You will learn more about creating unique customer experiences and processes as we go along.

Lets keep the momentum going.

You will need someone to fill out, stamp and address these mailers. I pay 20 cents per mailer to a local lady who does around 500-1000 mailers per week for me. She signs, stuffs, addresses and stamps each mailer.

Here are our expenses for mailing postcards

Cost of 1000 Cards = .4 cents each or $40
Cost of Postcard Stamps = .34 cents each or $340
Cost to Fulfill = .20 cents each or $200

For $600 we can have better odds than playing the lotto.

<u>If you do not have a lot of money but have time</u>, I recommend getting into the streets and going after distressed homes. I recommend nicer areas where distressed homes are easy to determine. Doing this in a war zone, seems like every property is in distress.

I LOVE HUNTING DEALS this way! I get so much done. I am able to gauge the market, find sellers, buyers and lenders this way. **Take a yellow pad of paper, a blue ink pen and start writing address and notes of properties to research them on the county website to find out who the owner is and mail them telling them you are interested. While you are there, leave a note on the door for them to call you.**

It's not uncommon for me to spend a full Saturday or Monday in the streets looking for deals. At the end of the day, I research all my leads, put any conversations into a database for future contact/follow up, mail the properties I found to be distressed and wait for the calls to come in. After a few weeks of doing this, you will have built a great pipeline that eventually begins avalanching deals into your lead system.

(Side Note - Technology has made this process very simple and you can now do this in a matter of minutes instead of days. Use the www.GoDrivingForDollars.com app to your advantage). I still leave notes on the door, even when using the app to collect addresses.

Plan to mail them for the long haul. **It will take an average of 6 campaigns for your market just to recognize your name**. Keep following up. I could write another book on follow ups.

My rule of thumb for following up is we follow up until we buy it or someone else does. Period.

When someone calls to say, "Erik, I get it. You want to buy my property. I know cause I have been receiving your cards for years. Please remove me and when I want to sell, I'll let you know."

I am glad to let them know I will remove them because now I have a phone number I can text and say, "Hey, its Erik. Do you still own the property at 123 XYZ?" True story. It works.

The whole purpose of this process is to determine your most motivated sellers in your farm area and begin getting in front of them in multiple ways. The more sellers you add to your list of contacts, the more your chances increase of creating an opportunity.

For instance, in one farm area, we might be mailing

ALL of the distressed properties in that area

All of the properties inherited in that area

Properties with specific zoning characteristics like Single Families that have allowed for multi family properties.

Our Top 100 property list

These are just a few instances of highly probable scenarios that we market to. Each of them is spoken to in a completely different language, none of which says, "We Pay Cash in 3 Days, Look At Me, No Repairs, No Costs". We have taken a different savvier approach and even for the deals we are willing to pay cash for, it mentions nothing about paying cash in 3 days. The message is tailored to say something similar, with there being more emphasis on the benefits to them.

Action Steps from Chapter 2

Determine if you will use time to generate leads or spend money to generate leads

If you plan to use your time, focus on building your list of the most likely candidates who will sell you their property. Since you plan on putting in the street time, focus on collecting 1000 addresses of distressed properties and doing all you can to get in contact. Leave a note, mail a postcard and make it a point to get creative in reaching your audience. Our workshops are great places to learn this process.

If you plan to spend money, I recommend starting at your local GIS department for data. They are second inline to working with the cities to keep information as accurate as possible.

Focus on the RESULT not on the OUTPUT

Remember, direct mail is a long term consistency game. Don't begin doing direct mail if you don't plan to mail more than 5 times.

Make it a goal to get at least 100 letters/postcards/notes out each week. If possible, make it 1000. Just don't ever go one week without sending messages to your list of opportunity.

CHAPTER 3

How Many Leads Did You Capture This Week?
How Many Appointments Did You Go On This Week?

This is where the rubber meets the road in this business.

You must have lead-flow and **you must be having face to face meetings with buyers, sellers and lenders of real estate.**

Truth told, the websites, your Facebook update, your online advertising all take a second seat to getting daily face to face meetings with buyers, sellers and lenders.

This is what all of your effort leads up to. This moment right here!

Most of our coaching calls begin with these two main questions.

Why?

This is what truly matters if we want to get to the closing table.

Leads = Appointments

Appointments = Offers

Offers = Closings

Closings = Freedom

You can see why everything else is just expensive entertainment if these basics are not being met.

Use your discretion to determine if someone wants retail. Be ok being the guy who needs to buy at fair market value. Do you know how many appointments we have went on that the seller had high expectations that we couldn't live up to?

The great thing was, we only lived up to what we could promise and when the rest of the market didn't live up to her expectations, she came back to do business with us do to our character and confidence in what we do.

Don't spend all day in retail appointments, but make an appearance, put your best foot forward and let them know you are grateful for the opportunity and the door is always open to revisit the conversation if it doesn't work out how they want.

This can be painful as you will be wanting to take these deals down, however you can only put your best foot forward and leave it right there for them to decide.

These appointments will arm you with the confidence to be ready for the real thing when you finally get a motivated seller.

Rather than think of these as appointments, which many people get overwhelmed and paralyzed by, lets replace it with "real estate conversations and questions of proposition".

My mentor, Greg Pinneo drilled into my head that ALL of my conversations should be concluded with a question of proposition.

What that means is, whether I am at a garage sale or intense negotiation, It is my duty to learn all art forms of negotiation by listening intently for the unheard and putting questions that require a yes or no answer in front of my audience.

It's my new language. Not just in real estate, but everywhere.

Its scientific. Those questions reveal key points of information that help you provide real value and relief from property owners.

Not all sellers need financial relief from the sale of the property. They want the burden lifted.

Call on FSBOs, FOR RENT signs, call wholesalers on all the bandit signs, stop and ask neighbors that are out walking, talk with landscapers and mail men (we once purchased a portfolio of homes from a family that came from a mail man lead). These people spend their lives in the streets and know more about vacant houses than most.

Get in the habit of these casual conversations, so when you do get into the real opportunity with someone who may be a little pushy, you're able to keep your cool and provide value to their underlying frustration.

Make habit of turning casual conversations into opportunities that compound your ability to find out relevant information.

This doesn't have to always be so formal or suit and tie style meetings.

My wife loves to garage sale. Whenever I go with her, I have made it common practice to ask how the sale is going and begin working my way into finding out whats going on with the property.

Are they downsizing?

Settling an estate?

Thinking of renovating?

Very causal. Non invasive. No threat here.

Its these types of casual conversations that lead to unexpected opportunities.

When they respond back and say, "yeah, our mom just passed and dad is going to be moving in with us so before we have to deal with probate, we are going to be selling the house. It's a lot of work getting this cleaned up and having to think of dealing with contractors and realtors".

That is a lead. A GREAT LEAD.

No one knows about it. You're on the inside of it and you have crucial information about it.

Depending on how that conversation is going and if they are not overwhelmed with dealing with people at the garage sale, I might throw out "I'd be interested in giving you an offer. Mind showing me around the inside?"

Otherwise I usually buy something so they can tie me to one of the items and then I will mail a thank you card and say...

Linda,

It was great meeting you at the garage sale on Saturday. Thank you for the great deal on the Scrabble game. We had some good laughs that evening with our family. Also, I recall you mentioned that the property (never use the word "Home") may be going up for sale soon. I didn't want to intrude further that day, however I would be interested in presenting an offer when the time is appropriate.

Please let me know if you need any help with repair men, dumpsters, tradesmen and the overwhelm that comes from these situations. We are here to help even if we don't buy the property.

Thanks again.

Erik

The great thing about casual conversations like this, is that they are not salesy or invasive.

Its two people having a casual conversation about a real life situation that you can shed some light on.

Like two friends talking.

Often times, this is where we pull sellers "off the market". Although it's not official that they are selling, when it does come time, you are getting that phone call.

Just think if you were armed with a few honest casual conversations like this each week. Focused lists make these conversations very possible.

The truth of the matter is, the right letter or postcard, can lead you to casual conversations that increase your chances of getting to those meetings.

These face to face meetings get you away from behind the computer screen (which most people don't realize), blocks our sensors from wanting to speak face to face to people. **Keep in mind that all phone calls are supposed to do is get you the face to face meeting.**

DO NOT TRY TO CLOSE THEM ON THE PHONE.

Get personal.

This is truly an art. Just be YOU-nique. Don't be a big shot who claims to buy up everything. Try being the small guy. The underdog, the normal everyday hard worker who is looking for a fixer upper in the neighborhood.

Keep a yellow pad with notes on all your appointments and follow up with all of them each month. **You are 10x more likely to close a deal from someone you have already made contact with than you are from a new lead. Know That!**

Make it a healthy habit to have as many daily face to face appointments with potential buyers, sellers and lenders of real estate.

I also recommend sending a Thank You card after every meeting you ever have. Go to the dollar store if you have to and buy a pack of 10, silver foil Thank you cards and drop them in the mail at the nearest mailbox after every appointment.

These Thank You cards have been an incredible untapped source of deals for us, simply because we were already there for the meeting, but despite feeling as if we had the deal locked down, this card solidifies our gratitude to be considered. Many times winning the deal over.

Action Steps For Chapter 3

Start tracking the leads you receive back each week or month. Know if they are calls, emails, text, website opt-ins or pre recordings.

Then, begin tracking how many of those leads are required to get an appointment. These key profit indicators will mean a lot one year from now as you begin to see how many leads it takes to get a deal.

Role play with a trusted friend who will give you honest feedback about your "casual conversation" and your "questions of proposition".

Begin calling on For Rent signs, bandit signs, For Sale By Owner signs, visit garage sales and do all you can to begin having these conversations with buyers, sellers and lenders of real estate.

Create index cards with your perfected script

Rehearse that script until it becomes unrehearsed

Stay mindful of your ratios.
How many conversations lead to a lead?
How many mailers lead to a call?
How many calls lead to an appointment?
How many appointments lead to an offer accepted?
How many offers lead to a closing?

CHAPTER 4

Making Intelligent Offers That Stick

One of the most frustrating things I deal with from newcomers and seasoned pro's is how much time they spend on finding deals and then when they do, **they don't write an offer.**

They say:

The seller wanted too much
The seller wouldn't have accepted it
The seller said they were gonna keep it now
The seller said they have an offer already
The seller said their friend is a realtor

The seller is really saying....**nobody has provided enough value for me to say, YES I WILL SELL TO YOU. Thats what they really mean when they say any of the above.**

Less than 3 sellers have ever came right out and said *"I need to liquidate and will take whatever you give me"*. And those houses were nothing to write home about.

In a great neighborhood IT'S NEVER HAPPENED.

Most sellers set a base price in which they have no logical, provable or verifiable justification as to why it is that price. Often times it's a high mark of something that sold locally, that is not truly comparable.

Then its up to you to get somewhere close to that or have realistic justification as to why you are offering what you are offering. **BUT WRITE THE OFFER if you take the time to meet with any seller.**

One of my friends and mentors, Mike Cantu who has bought over 2000 properties in his time told me that 50% of his buying came from giving an offer to every seller, even those who said he was competing with other offers.

Even if they said "no" now and other investors are still waiting to buy, most investors give verbal offers which means nothing.

Side Note: I cannot stress this enough, but follow up follow up follow up. Sellers can hang up the phone with you and then go have lunch with a friend that shares a nightmare story on their tenants and now they want out, Today! That's human psychology. When you follow up, DON'T BADGER THEM. Find a way to bring value.

Looking at deals without writing an offer is like paying for a gym membership, showing up and not working out. Write the offer.

We usually write the sellers three separate offers.

One for all cash with a diligence period.

One for all cash with no diligence period.

One on owner finance where the seller will carry a note if they own free and clear.

Right now we are going to focus on your cash offers. We discuss owner finance in depth at our mastermind and online workshops.

Next, you have to **build yourself a nice presentation when presenting these offers.** The "in your face, bam, here is what it is" offer comes across as shock to property owners who all think their property is worth much more than the neighbors.

When I had a realtor writing 500 offers for me per month on REOs, it was emotionless and direct. Thats perfectly fine. When you are dealing with little Sally who has memories in her moms property, you need to put some consideration into it.

People do business with those they like, know and trust. I have bought several houses for less than our competition offered because of our likable approach and sensitivity towards certain situations.

I do have a little secret that I have sworn to live by when doing business with everyday property owners.

This has served us quite well in our 10+ years as real estate buyers.

Never make an offer, without first making a connection.

I have found that in having these casual conversations, there will be many great opportunities for you to lead a comment to an "on ramp" that fast tracks your relationship.

Could be something you share in common such as

A person you both know.

Similar place in the world you have both been.

Unique experience you both shared together.

A snapshot in time you both recall.

Be on the look out for these on ramps and use them genuinely to advance your rapport with property owners.

There have been many, many times when I would catch myself laughing with them and then you are reminded of why you are really here.

Thats when I'd say something like "Wow Linda, we have been having such a good time I almost forgot why I was here."

When you feel that commonality create a seamless bond between you both, thats when you know you have made a connection and therefore can make an offer.

I also have another secret that we use to keep the connection between us.

We want sellers to be comfortable with our offers and have a reason to understand why we are offering what we are offering.

These numbers are not just picked from the atmosphere and dropped on a piece of paper.

This is a mathematic equation, that if worked properly, in all fairness can reward you with some financial blessings and freedom.

Help them to understand what you have to go through in order to make this fruitful.

Here is how we present our offers to private owners. I created a template that was mainly fill in the blank but includes all the info laid out that just needed to be specific to their situation.

I include a nice cover letter explaining who we are, thanking them for the opportunity, the benefits of doing business with us and what to expect throughout this process. They are given our title reps name and contact number, the professionals who will be assisting us in the process and a general timeline of how this works.

I include comps of recent comparable sales they can verify. Now when doing comps, I generally remove the high comp and the low comp and focus on the sweet spot in the middle. We print these out in full color and highlight important facts on the comps like sold date, days on market, list price, sale price, agent remarks about the property that we must include if we want the same results, price per square foot.

Many people see this is really shooting yourself in the foot and yes its true, doing it this way will usually prevent you from "stealing" someones property. However, our goal is a fair deal and in todays market, transparency goes a very long way.

We also include a repair bid of what we will be doing to get the property back in order to receive top dollar from the market.

Lastly, we break down EXACTLY what they will walk away with if they decide to do business with us.

Beginning from the after repaired sale price, closing costs, payoffs, seeing our repairs, costs of holding the property, we wind up a net number that there is very little to argue about.

If it ever comes up that our proceeds (never use the word profit) seem a little high, we generally combat that with that being the best case scenario if everything goes the way we plan. We always follow that up with asking them if they would ever consider working for 40 hours and not getting paid.

This is usually a no brainer answer and then we remind them that this will take nearly 40-120 hours to get this to where it needs to be and that we have several families in our company who depend on our accurate judgement.

Although this is not their problem, this is all the reward we get for taking these risks.

It also serves as a reminder that they are perfectly capable to go fetch these margins on their own if they want to go through these hours to get these results.

Lastly, I include testimonials and references for them to contact as a sign of our stewardship.

I did this over time as I heard new objections from sellers.

On occasion I even went as far to show them what we stand to make if all goes right.

My goal was to eliminate the stumbling blocks people face when making these decisions. Offers can take up a lot of time so it is crucial to build this packet one time and fill in the blanks each time you have an offer to write.

The bottom line is, when you are taking time out of your life to look at property, why would you not follow up with a well written offer regardless of what the seller says about being at a certain price?

<u>**WRITE OFFERS** *or you cannot complain that there are no deals.*</u>

Action Steps For Chapter 4

Work on your unique process for creating a connection with your sellers.

Craft your ideal offer packet that you will present to property owners. This will include cover letter, 3-5 recent comparable sales, breakdown of repairs, how you arrived at the offer price, seller net sheet and testimonials. Each of these should be one page, easy to navigate and simple to understand. Lastly, follow the packet up with an actual written offer outlining the details of the deal. As an incentive, you can let them know if they are willing to commit right now, you will pay ALL closing costs.

<u>Download The Secret To Negotiation Report</u> to gain a little additional insight on how to walk sellers down the path to fruition.

Record and keep the offers you write. Save each file in a folder with a word doc version and pdf. Often times, deals have a way of coming back and this is great way to stay on top of the opportunity.

Know your ratios. How many offers to deals accepted are you averaging? This will be a great KPI to help you understand future marketing.

CHAPTER

5

Closing The Deal

"Dig a Well Before You Are Thirsty"

Funding is often the main concern for real estate entrepreneurs. Sure you can make a nice lifestyle out of assigning properties, however, you'll only ever be as good as your last month.

The goal is to get to become free through real estate investing, not trading hours for dollars. If at first you have to pay your dues to the piper, so be it.

Its worth it!

However, lack of funding often keeps investors at their entry level potential for the majority of their career.

If you are used to the word "wholesaling," this is almost an oxymoron, because wholesalers often find some of the best deals in the market and then turn around and hand them off to someone else for a fee that is a fraction of the wealth they would have just earned in equity.

Again, as a newcomer, this is paying your dues to the house. No pun intended.

Just know it doesn't have to be this way. There are lenders of all sorts who can fund your deals.

Transactional funding from $750 - $2500 per day

Short term hard money loans at 15%-18% interest

Rehab loans from 8%-12%

Long term investment loans from 4%-8%

Were going to talk about positioning yourself to begin borrowing money, establishing a track record and why now is the best time to begin building relationships with multiple lenders.

Lets discuss how you align yourself for attracting lenders.

Becoming a likable character is equally important as maintaining an investment that delivers a consistent solid return.

I know many people who are amazing investors and run incredible businesses, yet have a hard time cleaning up their etiquette to obtain that IT factor.

Its worth re-mentioning that people do business with those they know, like and trust. When you are a pleasure to talk with, understand the realities of risk and know your model well enough to help overcome any objections without getting defensive, you will have the formula for turning casual conversations into YES propositions.

Real estate is an incredible investment vehicle for secure returns because its proven, tangible and secure.

I know there is always so much emphasis on risk these days. Everyone is so concerned about placing their money into some asset or in the hands of someone else.

Honestly, from my perspective of doing well over 400 private loans, our lenders get paid really, really well. While I am still very aware that anything can happen, I feel as if I am a VERY good steward of that money that has been trusted to us.

I am confident in our investment strategy.

I am confident in our investments.

I am confident in our operations.

I am confident in our ability to hedge against a downturn.

It truly does not ever cross my mind what a default would be like.

Knowing that I can buy a house this morning for $82,000 and sell it this afternoon for $94,000 and pay you $1000 for loaning us the $82,000 for a day is a very good feeling of stewardship.

Or that we can buy a $350,000 property, give our lender 7% annual return on his money, secured by a first position mortgage on an incredibly located, performing asset that was purchased at 78% of market value, turnkey, is a great feeling.

I am able to take someone who is getting ripped off by the bank paying him .65% (thats just over 1/2 of 1%) and give him 7%.

And its secured by an incredible piece of performing real estate.

Therefore, since I am able, I am obligated.

It is my duty to let people know that the banks are ripping them off.

We provide excellent opportunities for investors to park money and grow their wealth.

These investors are all around us. Most of them do not drive Ferraris or live in mansions.

They are every day people who are equally looking for you, like you should be looking for them.

When I think of some of the lenders we use, they include

Attorneys

Business owners who own real estate

Title processors

Our buyers

Retired Army veterans (We actually found this guy off a bandit sign call. He called wanting to buy one of our properties. After meeting, he became a lender of ours.)

Those who have inherited some money and are willing to play with it.

Your gym is likely filled with everyday individuals who have capital to invest.

So just how do you borrow money when you have never bought a house before?

The answer in short is a GREAT deal and supreme confidence that you can accomplish what you agree to accomplish.

The reality for most investors, is that you'll likely assign your first few deals until you establish a track record or have a mentor/money partner help you fund and close the deal.

Perhaps a REIA president with a good understanding of the market can align funds for you in exchange for a small fee. This is how I did my first deal and my REIA president didn't even align funding or find a buyer. I literally did all the work, with very little guidance and still paid 60% of my profit. I'd do it all over again too.

Or a business owner who serves as a mentor to you will lend funds.

There are many variables that need to be done with precision to become a good borrower.

It makes sense to build a track record under yourself as you begin to establish these relationships.

Let them know of the deals you are finding.

More importantly, let them know how much the investor you sold it to is making.

Show them the numbers. Let them see the potential.

If you are finding really good deals, one of the greatest scenarios would be for many investors to want your deal and then you can reposition yourself to see who will begin lending to you.

We turned a few buyers into lenders this way. Just a simple repositioning from being the "wholesaler who finds the best deals to the wholesaler who is now maximizing more of them. However your buyer can still earn money lending to you and align themselves for the future deals you cant take on".

This becomes your rock solid track record. Do you see why you treat this business seriously?

Within your first five deals you can be perfectly aligned to begin borrowing money.

So what do you say when you meet these people?

Number one, NEVER ASK FOR MONEY.

What? Then how do you ever borrow peoples money if you do not ask?

You must **learn to offer opportunities** to secure their money with excellent collateral that pays consistent interest on asset backed real estate.

THEY NEED YOU.

Be casual in your conversation about what you do. Say something like, **"I capture equity through financial and physically distressed real estate situations. We add value and then make returns as high as 30% and pay our financial partners as much as 10% while offering security, collateral and some of the healthiest returns in the United States"**.

There is a lot of psychology in that paragraph.

If you feel you can live up to it, use it.

I Capture Equity - This creates a mysterious "add on" to what EXACTLY do you do? Most lenders are involved in the financial world and ALL want to know how to capture equity.

Financially and Physically Distressed - A highly profitable business model lenders are familiar and comfortable with.

We Add Value - This puts them at ease since they rely on you to add value to the market that drives sales and ultimately returns on their money.

Our Financial Partners Make as Much as 10% - This raises the eyebrow question...Well How Do I Become A Partner? Now the ball is in your court. You could pay people who have $500k or more 10% and everyone under $500k gets 8%. You set the bar now. They are interested in YOU getting them these same returns on their money. Be authentic, fair and slow to make commitments and you will increase your value in these situations.

While Offering Security, Collateral and Some of The Healthiest Returns in The U.S. - All lenders want security, collateral and red carpet service. Their stock broker is a joke. Most people think they get 6-8% from their investments and have no idea about the fees eating away their money.

This is where you move them into the soft close. As you continue to add more value to the conversation, roll this over to a case study or scenario you are comfortable speaking about. Something like...

"A typical deal we did last week...or just one made up in your mind if you have not done your first deal yet is purchased for $100,000, is worth $240,000 to the market, needs $65,000 in repairs and stands to make $50,000-$70,000 in profit". You then go on to lay out the plan and terms for borrowing money. "We borrowed 100% of the acquisition and remodeling funds from our lender, gave a first position mortgage, a promissory note, pre paid the insurance policy for one year and listed the lender as the loss payee and paid the lender his $16,500 in interest when we sold the property."

Then go on to...

"The unique character of deals like this is they have to be moved on immediately."

(If they are car guys, talk about a situation they can relate to.)

"Its like when a Ferrari comes to the showroom at $8,000 less than any other Ferrari you have looked at. You don't wait. You act. My partners know if they want solid returns and security, I have to have the confidence to act when we see an opportunity to capture equity."

How would you like for me to show you our next opportunity? Perhaps following along on that may help you understand the lifecycle and process of our model.

Do not go for the hard close.

This is how you offer your services and casually have people coming to you for more information.

Offer. Don't ask.

Side Note - Do not ever put yourself in a situation where you are "needy" for money. Building trust with your lenders takes a real relationship. You likely will not attend a Friday networking event and secure the money needed for Monday's closing. It will likely show in your presentation. Focus on providing value and offering your business model. When they see this level of casual confidence, they will be coming to you for more info. Make it easy to show them how easy it is for them to do business with you.

Action Steps for Chapter 5

Create a list of potential lenders you may already know. Lenders for fast cash deals, short term rehab deals and long term buy and holds. The criteria mentioned above is a great place to begin.

Create your vision and understand your business model. When you show up focused and clear, it shows confidence. By explaining that your first 5 deals will generate a $7000 assignment fee with the goal of the making the buyer a $32,000 rehab, let them know YOU want to be the guy capturing the whole $39,000 and therefore can pay the lender 10% for lending the money. Be clear and deliberate.

Meet with them and build rapport. If they are already lending, let them know you plan to buy many of these for yourself but wanted to know if they would also fund a deal for one of your buyers.

Use the mortgage, promissory note and payoff letter we gave you at the end of this book to show potential lenders the documents you use.

CHAPTER

6

Building Relationships With Buyers Who Know, Like and Trust You

"You Can Sheer A Sheep Many Times, Yet You Can Only Skin Him Once"
                                    Mike Cantu

Knowing your markets biggest buyers is crucial to your business. **Showing value and getting someone to want to do business with you is an art form**. **You have to learn to show value.** There are people who simply "forward" deals to other people and get cut out of the picture because they did not protect themselves or show any value.

I want to make my goal with you very clear.

My goal is for you to become a BUYER of real estate. Don't become known as a wholesaler or a seller.

With that said, there will be times when it makes sense to assign your rights to a deal for a nice profit.

You could be loaded up with projects, have a deal in an area you don't particularly invest in or just simply feel like taking a nice vacation and flipping this deal quickly.

Whatever the reason, you will want to have great relationships with your areas top buyers.

Don't ever view them as competition. Many of them are buyers of your deals and better yet, potential lenders on your deals.

I cannot stress enough how important it is to position yourself as a buyer of real estate, while having the confidence of knowing you can send a few text messages, have a casual conversation and assign your deal for a nice profit if you WANT to.

There is one universal secret to getting people to like you that will never change. Without it, you will struggle in all areas of life if you do not practice this and make it second nature.

Before I tell you, you need to know that you first off have to be real. If you're a phony, shallow, only interested-in-the-money person, your bank account will reflect it. *You have to be sincerely interested in other people.*

As an investor, wholesaler, husband, wife, employee or anything in life, you have to **have an authentic interest in the people in your life**. When I found a guy who was buying a lot of properties, I wanted to meet with them personally. Face to face.

I always prefer to meet at a property than over lunch. If you want to eat, grab subs and meet at a potential deal or even one of their projects. No time for small talk. Meet at a property and listen closely.

I was there to learn as much as I can about what makes them tick. What does their financial blueprint look like? What is their investment model? What do they buy? How much per square foot? Where?

I knew my business so well that I already know I can deliver the goods. **I needed to know how to deliver it to them.** I also became an open book to them. Need a referral for a handyman or skilled trade? No problem? Looking for an investor friendly title company? Use ours. It's not about sending them a house and sitting back and collecting a check like all the gurus talk about.

Those people get worked out of the industry every day. I want to share an adverse approach to flipping properties that is the exact opposite of what EVERYONE does. It has be designed to be risk free and simple if you put in the up front work.

Its about relationships and relationships grow when value is consistently present.

The typical way of flipping property is to find a deal, lock it up and then scramble to find someone to flip it to. At times, assigning properties can seem downright exhausting, and what you're trying to do is put money in someone else's pockets so many times you end up dealing with their greed, have to deal with their unorganized business practices.

There is another way and its just now become widely known about. Let me paint a picture for you. Have you ever talked with people who say they have 3000 people on their "buyers" list?

We do to. The funny thing is, we sell to the same 7 buyers. So why not focus on those 7 people and don't worry about the rest?

This is like putting the 80/20 rule into effect,

I meet with those 7 people regularly to find out what they are looking for and where.

Then we go shopping.

If I know a guy is well funded and ready to buy a few good flips, I will tell my agents I need deals in that area and build a marketing campaign to bring him exactly what they want. Now I am focused on a specific area and basically know that any call I get, I can sell to them for $125,000, so any thing I negotiate under that, is in our bank account.

Here is where this gets awesome.

Its adverse to finding a deal, putting it under contract, shopping it, having people come back at a lower price, making you have to go back and renegotiate and look dumb.

By doing it this way you have already pre sold your property so you know when your phone rings, you can give a base price right up front and then look at the repairs needed and know its already sold. No more guess work. Your basically packaging deals, putting it on a platter and have it sold.

Just like McDonalds takes your order and serves it up to you.

It's simple. So we keep it simple for them.

The greatest position you can ever place yourself in is to be a buyer of real estate. By establishing this level of confidence and understanding with your buyers, they know the boundaries have been set and it comes down to this.

You find great deals.

You're perfectly capable of closing them and profiting on your own.

You are willing to let some of them go to buyers who make it easy, don't complain about your fee and do what they say they will do.

The moment they violate that, they can go back to fighting over deals their realtor is bringing them that are not exclusive.

Create this understanding with your buyers. If their agent brought them a deal at $130,000 and you bring it at $120,000, not only do they not care about your fee, they are going to call you before their agent. THERE IS HUGE value in that. This is reverse engineering and works well ONLY if you have people skills to know how to really position yourself as anything other than a typical wholesaler.

Once you have buyers that move fast, pay cash and see the value, you can even back off mailing so much and begin reaching out to other wholesalers and agents and let them know you have a few fast moving, cash paying buyers and start selling their inventory. DO NOT JUST FORWARD DEALS.

Go get clean clear photos, put together a wholesale packet with photos, details, comps, maps, repair quotes and deliver on a platter. This is something you can have a virtual assistant do for less than $5 for each property. We've included one in the back of this book.

I assure you of this.

Today, people are LAZY. **Be better than them and your bank account will show. Look at your market, find out what is missing, build that service, sprinkle some value in there and begin selling these deals.** Our whole business shifted when we understood this principle. When you match it with a killer seller leads, there are HUGE paydays to be had. GET GOING

Action Steps for Chapter 6

Use your time in the streets to identify active buyers. By taking notice to dumpsters, contractor vans and rehabs going on, these are great ways to find "right now" buyers.

Know their numbers so you know how to present a deal to them. Research the deal to verify how much they paid for how many square feet and then determine price per square foot.

Approach them as a resource that can help them with areas they need resources for. Often times, they just want your deals. This is when you kindly let them know that you don't typically sell much (pure positioning), however if you do, here is how it works.

Don't tolerate any nonsense from them. If they try funny business, circumventing you or anything that is not ethical, kindly let them know that they have abused your friendship and therefore are no longer interested in pursuing a relationship.

The goal is always a fair deal.

CHAPTER

7

Growing and Scaling Your Real Estate Business

Growing a real estate business is an incredible experience. As we deal with new chapters, opportunities and situations, there will be times when you will feel a little overwhelmed by our circumstances.

This is natural with anything new we take on.

Especially when it is something that has the ability to radically improve our life. There are several exercises and resources in the back of this book to help you with that.

As you grow in this area you will recognize the value of being around other big thinkers. Having a sphere of influence where you can be vulnerable with your needs is an important step to identifying where you can improve and how to implement those steps as quickly as possible.

Where this can become toxic to many growing investors is the ability to look outside of our own vision and see a glimpse of what someone else is succeeding with and believing its easier over there.

I assure you, at some point, they put in an incredible amount of time to be able to get those "easy" deals.

Do not abandon your own vision for any reason.

I recommend making your vision so concrete that you confidently promote it in all that you do.

Perhaps not like a wacko marketing fanatic, but a subtle, ever so confident expression of what you are doing, that is felt at your core.

When you exude this passion, you may begin to notice more people who attract towards you due to this vision and confidence.

Stay true to yourself and make your own noise in life.

Once you have a clear vision, have written down your goals, determined your action plan to get you there, set a deadline to accomplish these goals, its time to begin aligning yourself with other like minded thinkers who you can bounce ideas off of and begin trading resources to help you scale your business.

Often times, this requires you to look outside of what is primarily available right in front of you.

I don't believe we would ever be here today had we chosen to stay in the realms of our local REIA events.

Nothing against REIAs, its just been my personal experience that big thinkers and major players don't generally hang out there.

<u>I recommend a business development or real estate mastermind.</u>

These are GREAT ways to grow and scale your business.

We offer a solid group of guys who meet several times per year to collaborate ideas, share opportunities and trade resources so can use our time together wisely and get the speed of implementation going as quickly as possible. You can find out more info and even send an application to be considered at SelfManagingFreedom.com

However, your mentors and masterminds should align with your core values and business goals.

Some people truly cannot help those in certain situations since they specialize in another.

For instance, in our mastermind you need to make a minimum of $100,000 in the last year to get in.

Why would we do something like that?

We have found those that we truly help the most are already running a successful business and earning at least $100,000 per year.

These business owners have often become capped by their own abilities. They NEED to learn how to scale their business and WANT to do so without them having to be the one who accomplishes everything in the future.

These are the perfect candidates for us to work with and show them how to implement systems, determine their key profit indicators so we can build processes that streamline how they service their customers and then we show them how to wrap it up in one amazing unique customer experience so they are consistently gaining market share without them having to consistently be the one who manages these tasks and processes.

Get in the habit of looking for those who can help serve you in business.

Don't be afraid to invest in yourself.

Also, don't follow the belief that throwing money at something will solve your problem. Put in work.

If you could pay $10,000 for one tip or idea that you could repeatedly use to make $10,000, would you do it?

What if it only paid you $1000, but your virtual assistant did it every time for you?

Look, investing in your business is the same as going to the gym and getting your gym membership and hiring a personal trainer.

You don't wake up the next day with muscles.

It's not that it becomes noticeably easier to get muscles.

You still have to show up and do the work.

The difference is you have someone next to you helping you get a result, FASTER than what you could have on your own.

I still pay $2500 for 30 minute calls with people who can help me achieve a result faster.

Avoiding this fact will only cheat yourself in the end. Invest in YOU.

I have some friends I went to school with who think its awesome we do real estate as a profession.

They also cringe when they hear how much we spend on education.

Those same friends are often between jobs and still living with friends in an apartment because their $80,0000 college education did not land them the job they wanted.

It didn't land them a job at all. Many of them were over qualified and therefore employers would only offer them $18 per hour when the career usually gets $30 per hour. So after 4 years of school, they went in a total different direction and are paying high interest on student loans that don't even serve the industry they are now looking for jobs in.

And people are quick to say real estate is a pyramid scheme.

You will always be your own best investment.

Don't cheat yourself.

Lets look at a few other ways you can scale your business.

I never like to count chickens before they hatch (that means count money before the closing happens), however planning for scale makes it easy when you know you have a coming pay day.

For instance, you might be getting ready to complete a deal that is going to bring you $10,000 in proceeds.

It would be wise to take some of those funds, and allocate it for scaling your business.

This doesn't mean going out and renting office space, hiring a full time in house assistant and having to provide health care.

However, this would be an appropriate time to invest in systems that allow you to streamline your efforts.

I first off recommend hiring a virtual assistant.

We have virtual assistants (Philippines or India based) for general tasks like research, pulling up property records and locating a list of potential leads online.

We also have another VA who cleans up all of our marketing lists. She is an excel wizard and does great work in a timely fashion. I can basically send an email at 4pm on Tuesday with a task and have it done by 10am on Wednesday when I open my email. She is based in Kenya Africa.

She also referred us to a web developer who helps us build multi page websites for cheap.

These are just examples of the VA's we use and you can find them on sites like www.Upwork.com.

www.VA4REI.COM offers VA's specifically for real estate although you cannot just hire by the task. You have to buy monthly time blocks.

I prefer Upwork since it allows me to deal direct with the team I create and only pay for the work they perform. There are many more sites where you can find good teams, however, you may be required to buy time blocks and they are good for so many days/weeks.

With Upwork, I can create a job description, set my filters for what qualifications they should have and the applications start coming in.

The great part is, I am not committed to a paying a salary. I may only need to spend $36 this week to take care of one simple task.

I generally work with people who have a 90% plus rating and they know exactly what to do with very little guidance from me, as long as I was clear.

I am able to see when they logged in to work on my project, verify their efforts through their screenshots and the best part is, Upwork takes a very small fee out of the total amount, so we are not paying a large markup to them for having the platform for VAs to work with us.

Since you are getting these services at 1/4 - 1/2 the price of what you would pay in the states and the work is truly exceptional, Im not complaining at the price since this is not an expense, but an investment in our company and our own personal time.

I also recommend you consider hiring a team based VA. What I mean by that is you will likely work with one VA on the day to day, however, if something should happen to them, there is another VA who is trained on the same tasks and has a screen log of activity that needs to be completed.

This is also known as pooling.

This way, you never skip a beat if a VA gets sick or has an extended leave.

Now I know what you may be thinking.

"Erik, I am just starting out in this. I don't have that much going. How can I afford a virtual assistant?"

The VAs we mention above are paid between $3 to $7 per hour and speak fluent english, have solid internet access and are truly great at the services they provide.

You will be amazed at how much a $6 to $8 per hour virtual assistant can remove from your plate each day.

When you are very clear in your description and explanation of the tasks required, I assure you that you will begin finding other areas that you can hire out to the well qualified team members.

These VAs are trained for your real estate business. Here are just some of the tasks they can handle for you.

Transaction Coordination - $5 to $8 (closing your deals).

Marketing and prospecting - $3 to $7 (sorting lists, researching property owners, collecting data, contacting property owners online).

Administrative tasks - $3 to $6 (setting appointments, emailing and calling for follow up reminders).

Web coding and site development - $6 to $12 (Website updates, adding properties, autoresponders, webforms, etc).

Sales calls and follow ups -$7 to $10 (Perfect for prescreening sellers, reaching out to buyers, calling FSBOs, For Rents, online listings).

Handling personal matters like setting a reservation for dinner this Friday with your spouse, finding out what events are around town for networking.

Handling social media accounts and posts- $2 to $8

There is truly nothing that these VAs cannot handle and many times, they do it better than we do. It's amazing how well trained and poised they are.

Its terrible that the human brain often tricks us into thinking we cannot afford these "luxuries".

When we look at it this way, **we cant afford not to hire them.**

Lets say, your plan is to cold call for one hour each day for leads. Problem is, you are anti cold calling material. You cringe at the thought of it.

As you look back at your activity for the week, you noticed you spent 1 hour doing this task, which is crucial to your bottom line.

Since it didn't get done, what is the potential impact of revenue lost from not committing to this?

$5000, $10,000+?

So lets say you hired a VA to cold call for one hour per day and gave very clear instructions on what they are to perform.

Lets say you paid them $10 per hour.

1 hour per day, at $10 per hour x 5 days per week is a grand total of $50 per week.

Lets say she added 6 leads to your data base and added 2 appointments to next weeks calendar.

The potential to pay for her next year of cold calling could stem from this one $50 investment.

Now lets compound it with this...

You now have 5 free hours each week that you are glad to have back and your confidence is up because you know the important tasks are being done.

How much are those 5 free hours worth to you, let alone the mental clarity you now have from knowing this task is getting done?

As a recap, the best way to scale your real estate business is surround yourself with big thinkers and invest in yourself by implementing systems and team members who immediately begin taking tasks off your hand and giving you back more time.

This time can be used to spend building more of your business, enjoying time with family and friends, allow you to absorb all the information at your mastermind event while knowing tasks are still getting completed.

One of the last great ways that will help you scale your business is to understand more of who you are.

Sometimes the hiring process can be difficult because we are unsure of exactly what we want or have trouble handing off tasks that we feel no one else can do properly except us.

This was me 100%, until my partner told me about Kolbe. Kolbe helped me understand my entrepreneurial uniqueness.

For example, when it came time for us to begin mailing probates, my Kolbe went to work in some great ways.

I did all the research, learned how to get the information, place it in a spreadsheet, figured out what letter we were going to send, on what date, with what frequency, determine how the calls would be screened and basically set up a complete system for mailing probates.

I can do this with vigor and create an incredible system that allows us to gain considerable market share year after year.

Where my Kolbe shows me that I fail miserably is taking this unique process and doing it over and over every week.

Ill sincerely let you down if you leave me in charge of this.

Im a 6-7-5-3 which means I am great at envisioning something, brainstorming its creation, outlining the process, building the model, testing it and then tweaking along the way to make sure it's operating at full capacity.

It's the same reason I can look at someones business and identify hidden profit centers, show them where to increase revenues and create systematic processes that remove them from being the operator in their business.

However if I do not find someone to be the weekly operator of our probates and do all the tasks required to get them out each week, our probates would die their second week cause I get bored doing the same task over and over.

It's not a bad thing. It's actually been one of the greatest revealing characteristics I have ever discovered about myself.

All this time I just thought I sucked. Now I know its my Kolbe telling me that my MO (modus operandi) was never wired to include this part in my entrepreneurial uniqueness.

By understanding your Kolbe, you'll understand how to hire your Kolbe Right Fit. This is a person who has strengths where you are weak.

The last thing you want is two people who are great at completing the same tasks.

[Go to kolbe.com](http://kolbe.com) and take your Index A test. It costs $50 and will give you a full color, in depth report at what your entrepreneurial strengths are and which aren't.

As you get to know more about your Kolbe, you'll quickly pick up on other peoples strengths and recognize those opportunities to build your team based on how you see them perform in their current space.

Use this to your advantage and observe people you can bring onto your team.

Action Steps for Chapter 7

Take a moment and think big. Whatever initial profit you planned to earn this year, multiply it by 10. However many deals you planned to do this year, multiply it by 10.

Locate a few real estate events and masterminds to immerse yourself in those where you feel you will be challenged the most. Commit to joining one of them as quickly as possible. I recommend not waiting until you cash your first check.

Be willing to be vulnerable with your mentors. They can only help you to the level that you let them know what you need help with.

Consider hiring a VA. Maybe before your first deal. At the very least, create a Upwork.com profile and post a job description for whatever tasks you are not excited to perform. This way you will see why you actually cant afford not to hire a VA.

Take your Kolbe Index A test and study your results.

CHAPTER 8

Bonus Chapter
The Most Important Chapter of All...
The Real Secret to Your Success

I am so grateful for the time we have been able to spend together. This is only the beginning of our incredible journey together.

Im sure there are a lot of ideas and thoughts roaming through your head right now.

I'd like to share one of the stories I was having with my mentor, Greg Pinneo.

Not only is Greg a maverick in the real estate arena, he is also an avid pilot, adventurer and mountain climber.

During one of our discussions we were talking about a new course of action for our business. One that Greg implemented long ago and was still serving him until this day.

As we dug deep into implementing this, the over whelm set in.

I made a comment like "can't we just download this to my teams brain and our computer systems and it will all be done"?

Greg paused for a moment and shared an incredible principle about mountain climbing.

When Greg began climbing mountains, there were many new tasks that had to be accomplished.

There was the application to be considered for the climb.

The gear required to complete the journey.

The multiple times he had to complete a certain altitude of climbing within 6 months of the actual summit and a whole list of largely inconvenient items that MUST be accomplished or you simply cannot go.

So as Greg prepares for his summit, he learns that during the actual climb, he will have to begin at basecamp, climb up 3000 feet, descend back down 2500 feet, camp for the night, then the next day, climb up 5000 more feet, turn around and descend back down 3500 feet. And this is the pattern they commence to until they reach the summit on the last day.

Now Greg is an adventurer at his core (Cor is actually the name of his company), so it excited Greg to have all these challenges and Greg is the guy who likes to understand what he didn't know before so during the instruction class, Greg asked "why is it that we have to ascend and descend so many times throughout this journey"?

The instructor acknowledged Greg and said, "Great question! As a business owner, you'll be able to relate to this. As with any grand achievement, and especially true in mountain climbing, **you must acclimate your body to be able to handle the pressure. If you attempted to climb to the top in one climb, or we dropped you at the top from a helicopter, your body would simply implode due to the pressure of the atmosphere**"

That metaphor stands true for your life as well.

If I can send a download to your brain with all the info, you would implode from all the pressure.

Very similar to those who hit the lotto and have never had the responsibility of handling that amount of money, what happens? 87% implode from the pressure and end up dead, in jail, in lawsuits and broke within 5 years.

My whole point is this.

You want more for life or else you wouldn't be reading this book.

I'd love to magically wave my hand over you and make you a success. We both know that wouldn't work.

However, we offer the training and you have in your grasp, all the tools and conditioning you need to acclimate yourself and get you to the top of the summit.

I would like to begin telling you about the greatest secret to success I have ever been told (and also witnessed first hand).

Sure people will say things like "vision," "a team," "access to deals and private money".

These are all great ideas and strategies that play a role in success.

The only truth I have ever heard regarding the real secret to success came from a billionaire that I am very fortunate to spend time with almost every day.

I know him through some philanthropy contacts and he happens to be one of the largest independent landlords in Florida.

When I asked him the biggest contributor to his success is, he never even broke a stride, turned to me with a smile and said, **"I took massive action!" My first 35 months of living in South Florida, I bought 36 properties. That set the tone for me to buy double the amount the next 35 months."**

The biggest vision in the world is nothing without action.

The greatest team ever created means nothing without action.

All the leads and private money is purposeless without action.

Now I give credit to anyone who has amassed such a fortune. He surely has something incredible about his ability to perform.

However I am not awestruck by the fact that he is a billionaire, although he is the first person I ever met that put it to me straight. I have so much respect for what he teaches me and interestingly enough, it's directly opposite of what many other educators have taught me along the way.

MASSIVE ACTION

MASSIVE ACTION

MASSIVE ACTION

Everything in your life comes down to these two words right here. It doesn't matter if you're talking about this book, your relationships, your work ethic, your workouts...everything comes down to a choice to do nothing or take massive action.

I want you to take massive action towards your success.

Each chapter has a series of action steps that will get you closer to freedom with each new activity.

Start by going through chapter one and taking action to begin generating leads.

Leads are the lifeblood of your real estate business.

The best return on your time (and investment) in the real estate business is spent generating leads and converting them to fruition.

Don't let anything get in your way.

Don't be sidetracked because something is not perfect. You don't have to get it perfect, you just have to get it going.

If there is something you need that is not found in this book, on our resources page, online somewhere, just simply ask me for it.

Find me on social media and say, "Erik, Im taking massive action like you said and feel like I am being held up by this one thing, do you know where I can get this?"

We'll be there to help.

I don't claim to have all the answers.

Even after we paid for mentors and masterminds, we still had to create it from scratch (through massive action). We didn't care.

Massive action becomes easy when you have guidance, a road map and someone to help you get a result faster than you can get it on your own.

I am committed to your success.

Commit to taking massive action and we'll surely see each other along the way.

In the back of this book and in the online digital copy you will find several links to useful resources that will help you take massive action and get results faster.

Your future success is revealed in your daily routine.

CONCLUSION

So Here Is What This Boils Down To. These Action Steps Will Put You On The Fast Track To Doing Your First Deal (or The Next One), Increasing Your Income, Improving Your Life and Lead To Massive Growth…

1. Find Your Farm Area
2. Find 1000 Addresses
3. Leave Notes Behind and Mail The Owners
4. Call Every Realtor Sign While Driving And Tell Them You're Buying
5. Talk With Neighbors, Mailmen, Landscapers and Business Owners and Tell Them You're Buying Property
6. Call Every Wholesaler In Town and Get To Know Their Model
7. Keep A Yellow Pad of All Your Activity With Names, Addresses, Phone Numbers and Details of The Discussion
8. **Follow Up With These People Often**
9. Keep Building This List Forever
10. **Go On DAILY Face to Face Meetings**
11. Hunt For Buyers, Sellers and Lenders EVERY DAY
12. Ask questions of proposition
13. **Write Offers On Every Property You Meet At**

14. Follow Up
15. As You Grow and Deals Start Closing, Find a Helper To Help You Send More Mailers
16. Hire a Mentor
17. Get Educated
18. Spend More Time In The Streets
19. Watch Your Yellow Pad Come Alive

Do these action steps EVERY DAY and you will see the results. There is still much to learn on this journey BUT FIRST, **start with these action steps EVERY DAY.**

Once you have a firm grip on these, focus on improving your marketing to deliver greater responses, then work on negotiation so you can convert more leads to deals.

Once you have mastered this, move to building systems and processes that consistently market for deals the way you do without you having to do the doing.

Little by little you will see growth and scaled results and before you know it you went from standing on the sidelines searching for a way to get into real estate in to owning a secret portion of the market that no one can figure out how.

RESOURCES

In the following pages I am going to be giving you a lot of resources that have been a major help along the way.

Aside from the typical real estate resources like links to useful sites and documents, I am going to include some mind hacks, resources to remove friction from your life, goal planner worksheets and every resource that has helped me along my journey. It is my hope that you download the digital copy of this book and use this library to your advantage.

I assure you, we have invested heavily in these resources you are receiving for free and

9 Words to NEVER Use When Talking With A Seller

I am stupefied when I hear how so many investors talk. I call so many bandit signs around town, call all the mailers that the sellers give us when we buy their property. I can't imagine anyone ever taking a deal down the way I hear some people talk, let alone get to the point of buying properties in A class neighborhoods.

Here are some common words I hear people say all the time that you should ***never*** use and the words you should replace them with. You literally need to remove these from your vocabulary when talking with sellers.

Investor - Use the word builder, property owner or property buyer. Use handyman with a hammer if you need to. ANYTHING but investor. Those guys are right up with car salesmen.

Fast Cash - Try to move away from being a fast cash buyer. I have never met a seller who truly needs cash in three days and this usually scares them. Take it slow and push for the owner financing. If they want all cash, I still paint the picture that this will be settled in about 30 days although if they need it sooner, then we make it happen. Just begin moving yourself away from being the fast cash guys. In the savvy world of A class neighborhoods, fast cash means you're an amateur.

Profit - Use the word margin. Most people understand you need to have a margin for yourself. No wants to be profited from.

Wholesale - Use And/Or Assigns. If they ever ask what this means, tell them it's a protection clause that allows you to bring in a partner in the event you get hit by a bus but generally means you just have not determined which company name it will go into.

Qualify - I once heard an investor say they need to qualify them before they meet. My mouth dropped. Instead of qualifying, I use the word discover.

Execute The Contract - Seriously? Who wants to be executed? Tell them we need to "ok the agreement".

Steal - Get comfortable with the language of a fair market value. The definition of fair market value is the price a buyer and seller agree upon.

Offer - Instead of writing an offer, tell them you will be drafting a proposal. Proposals are harmless.

Offers open up the door for the seller to receive more offers.

Home - Use the word property. Do not use house, home or anything that inspires emotional triggers.

Make this your new vocabulary and you will see the impact you have in your casual conversations.

Practice and role play them.

Real Estate Documents and Spreadsheets

Simple 2 Page Purchase Agreement
Simple 2 Page PA

Option Agreement
Option To Purchase

Assignment Agreement
Assignment of Contract

Flex Option Agreement
Flex Option To Purchase Wholesale Deals

Private Mortgage, Note and Payoff
Example Mortgage
Example Payoff
Example Prom Note-1

Wholesale Packet
Wholesale Packet

Wholesale Pre Qual Form
Wholesale Buyer Prequalification Form

Daily Loan Interest Calculator
Daily loan calculator

Income/Offer Calculator
Erik Stark's calculations

Monthly Income Calculator
Monthly rental income

Profit Flip Calculator
Profit Expense Calculator

Rental Income Calculator
Rental-Income-Expenses-Template

Deal Journal (Best HomeStudy Course You'll EVER HAVE Is Of Your Own Deals)
Deal Journal Template.docx

Build Wealth Through Real Estate
Wealth Building Infographic.pdf

Seller Call In Lead Interview Sheet

Scripts for talking with buyers

Example of An Answering Service Script

Seller Marketing Cash Map
Seller Marketing

Brain Hacks

I keep many of these little brain hacks around in my journals, on flash cards and close by to help out when I get overwhelmed. I have learned that my emotions are completely negotiable and I possess the ability to manipulate them at will with the proper tools that can bring greatness back into focus.

Use them.

They work.

The Freeze Frame
From Doc Lew Childre

1. Learn to set defaults in your mind to recognize when you become frustrated. Use this recognition to call a time out.
2. Pull your focus away from your distress call (emotions and racing thoughts) and focus on the area around your heart. Now focus on your breathing. Feel the 6 second inhale and the 4 second exhale from your diaphragm
3. Recall a happy place or happy thought and relive it. A snapshot of peace, a feeling of joy, an overwhelm of belly laughter.
4. Bring that feeling to the present moment and ask your heart felt joy to take precedence over your mind filled emotions
5. Recognize your awareness to bring attention to your situation and your willingness to overcome the chaos.

How to Never Worry a Day In Your Life
Dale Carnegie

1. What am I worried about?
2. What can I do about it
   a. Get the facts
   b. Analyze the facts
   c. Act on your decision

"Confusion is the chief cause of worry"
"Worries usually evaporate in the light of knowledge"

How to Further Eliminate Worry in Business
1. Stop reciting the problem
2. Any problem presented must have 3 solutions
   a. What is the actual problem?
   b. What are three solutions to the immediate problem?
   c. How can we prevent this from occurring again?

"A clear, definite decision acted on is already 60% complete"

Creating an NLP Diverter
by Eben Pagan

Emotionally reframing negative energy is controlling your "meta state".

"Wrap" negative emotions with a positive outcome to change future reactions.

"Stack" positive powerful emotions to deliver a euphoric enact-ion.

Rather than be depressed about having lost out on a deal, remain confident that you are one step closer to a yes.

By focusing on the positive result, not the negative input, you can change your meta state.

NLP Training - The Study of Human Excellence

Change your mental coding on how you think and react to situations by reliving and focusing on the positive outcome.

Regardless of how frustrated you are, recite your statement in the positive. Always state what you want, not what you want to avoid.

Think of your most happy moment of happy place. Draw it close. Relive it for a burst of energy anytime. This is how you neuro-code your brain.

What you resist will persist, but what you focus on will expand.

Live, pray and affirm with your head up, not down. Shake off frustration and shout your way to happiness (Priming for greatness).

Create your own "Confidence Circle" with positive energy, photos of great times, laughter and anchor those thoughts to step into them at any time, free from the worlds frustration.

Replace distorted images of success with your envisioned photos of success. Internalize them and they will become and naturally attract.

Develop a "toward" motivation and happily work toward your big breakthrough instead of away from what you don't want that always leads to breakdowns.

Fear Setting
by Tim Ferris

1. What is the worst thing that can happen?
2. What can I do to minimize the possibilities of this happening?
3. What will it take for me to bounce back if this occurs?
4. Can I live with that scenario?
5. Make your decision.
6. Act on it.

Big Idea Goal Planner

Project 1: _____ **Project 2:** _____ **Project 3:** _____

5 items I must do to push this project further: 5 items I must do to push this project further: 5 items I must do to push this project further:

1: _____ 1: _____ 1: _____

2: _____ 2: _____ 2: _____

3: _____ 3: _____ 3: _____

4: _____ 4: _____ 4: _____

5: _____ 5: _____ 5: _____

Relationships: People I need to Contact today.
Make a list of the people you must reach out to today to assist or help keep accountable to this project

1.
2.
3.
4.
5.
6.
7.
8.

Accomplishments/ Priorities:
Make a list of the main tasks I must complete each day.
This is a list of to-do's and must accomplish items of importance. Do not put this list off, what goes on goes off completed.

1.
2.
3.
4.
5.
6.
7.
8.

Spend The Most Time, On The Few Things, That Make The Biggest Difference

Screenshot this page and print as needed

Productivity Hacks

Here are a few super simple outlines you can use to tackle big projects, map out ideas and make taking massive action easier. Use them to your advantage and use them often to minimize the brain damage of your new innovations.

B.O.R.E Outline -Procrastination Killer
By Dean Jackson

Rather than making a To Do list that often time leads to overwhelm and none of the items being accomplished, use this outline to take each project and break it down into consumable pieces that validate your next step.

Brainstorm - Take a few moments and "brain dump" everything that comes to mind regarding this project. Hold nothing back. Let it all out. The goal is to let all that consumes your mind about this come out on paper.

Outline - Take the best ideas from your brainstorm and create an outline of the most important topics you came up with. Only the best need apply and the clarity from the brainstorm will easily outline the action steps you'll be taking next.

Record - Now you are ready to begin "the doing". Take your outline and construct it one pillar at a time. Whether it's a newsletter, new postcard to test or blog post to write, it will come together easily if your outline was constructed properly.

Edit - Revise your final piece for optimal performance. The great part about doing it in these steps, is you can continuously tweak the end result by tweaking the outline to include your new found facts or process and jump right to editing, therefore implementing the changes immediately.

Free Reports

These free reports are like a home study course packed into a few short chapters and offer big ideas and quick implementation to help you begin making money in real estate faster.

The Secret to Marketing Most Investors Will Never Know About

The Secret to Negotiating Most Investors Will Never Know About

The Secret to Success Most Investors Will Never Know About

7 Ways in 7 Days To Find Buyers in Any Market

Real Estate Investing Rockstars...Insight from 29 of the Nations Top Investors

Lets be friends shall we...

Personal Facebook Page
https://www.facebook.com/theerikstark/

Personal Instagram
https://www.instagram.com/theerikstark/

Real Estate Hacks Instagram
https://www.instagram.com/realestatehacks/
You'll want to connect with us here for our weekly live discussions where we give out simple strategies to make money and you can ask us any questions.

Join The Faceless Leaders discussion here
https://www.facebook.com/ErikandSteve/
You'll want to connect with us here for our weekly live discussions where we give out simple strategies to make money and you can ask us any questions.

Cut Your Learning Curve, Increase Your Lead Flow, Improve Your Lead Conversion, Learn How To Maximize Your Deals, Make Big Money With Small Lists And Simply Do Bigger Deals With Less Headache And Live The Real Estate Investor Lifestyle…

Here are a few simple ways to work with us and get faster results in your business.

Ala Carte Professional Services

50 Minute Business Detox Session

- Eliminate Bottlenecks In Your Business **(Turn Bottlenecks Into Breakthroughs)**
- Discover Hidden Opportunities In Your Current Model **(Implement Those Opportunities)**
- How to Increase Profits **(Position Yourself To Receive Higher Paydays)**
- Outsource Undesirable Sources of Income **(Focus On Biggest Checks, Outsource The Rest)**
- How To Implement Magnetic Marketing Into Your Business **(Surely Your Competitors Are NOT Currently Doing This)**
- Get Clear On Where You Generate Your Greatest Sources of Revenue **(Know Your KPIs, Duplicate The Process and Design Unique Experience Around These)**
- Recorded Call For Future Listening **(You're Sure To Catch Something You Missed The First Time)**
- This Also Includes 30 Minutes of Intake/Discover/Review of Your Business **(Anyone Who Can Provide Answers Without Knowing Your TRUE Problems Is Committing Malpractice)**

My Guarantee: If You Feel That The Call Is Not Worth Your Money In The First 20 Minutes, I Will Refund Your Money In Full And You Get To Keep Everything Up To That Point.

Investment In Yourself - $297

Apprentice for a Day (Spend a Day In Our Market)

- Witness The Daily Practices That Are Crucial For Successful Real Estate Investors **(3 Items Every Successful Investor Is Looking for Everyday)**
- Learn The Art of Negotiation **(How To Ask A Few Questions And Learn Everything You Need To Perform At Your Best)**
- How Successful Investors Position Themselves **(In Every Conversation, Even Those Not Business Related)**
- Receive Hands On Knowledge On Real Live Deals We Are Working On
- Learn How To Handle Yourself When The Unexpected Happens **(Its Not How You Act, Its How You RE Act)**

*This is a HANDS ON Experience and You WILL be Placed Outside Your Comfort Zone (Live Calls, Live Meetings, Real Negotiations, Direct Questions of Proposition)

My Guarantee: If You Feel That You Are Not Receiving Your Moneys Worth By Mid Day Noon, I Will Refund Your Money And Everything You Have Received Up To That Point Is Yours To Keep.

Investment In Yourself - $2500

A Day In Your Market (Or Office)

- See Your Market Through The Lens of A High Level Real Estate Investor
- Discover Unforeseen Paydays You May Drive Past Every Day
- Why Ground Level Investing Is CRUCIAL In ANY Market **(Learn These Principles And You'll Adapt In ANY MARKET Condition or Location)**
- Challenge Your Thinking To Operate BIGGER and Learn The Language of Sophisticated Real Estate Investors
- This Includes Making Live Calls, Meeting People Face to Face And Stirring Up Activity That Very Well May Result In A Instant Payday

*This is a HANDS ON Experience and You WILL be Placed Outside Your Comfort Zone (Live Calls, Live Meetings, Real Negotiations, Direct Questions of Proposition)

My Guarantee: If You Feel That You Are Not Receiving Your Moneys Worth By Mid Day Noon, I Will Refund Your Money And Everything You Have Received Up To That Point Is Yours To Keep.

Investment In Yourself - $3000

Two Day Mastermind

- Engage With High Level, Like Minded Entrepreneurs in A World Class Environment
- Dig Deep Into Whats Working In Real Estate RIGHT NOW (Marketing, Deal Structuring, Negotiation)
- Learn How To Position Yourself As The Expert Buyer and Increase Your Paydays
- Discover The New Economy Way To Market Your Services That Your Competition Isn't Using

- Why Knowing Your Entrepreneurial Identity is The Single Most Important Principle That Determines Your Success - Or Accelerates Your Failure
- Hot Seat Session With Big Three Ideas for Your Business and The Strategies/Team to Implement Them in The Next 14 Days
- Leave With A CLEAR Strategy On How To Reposition Yourself

Apply Here (www.SelfManagingFreedom.com)

Review A Deal

- Want An Expert Set of Eyes On Your Next Deal To Make Sure You Are Maximizing Your Return?
- Discover The Potential Pitfalls Before They Happen
- Learn How To Control The Overpriced Leads You Keep Stockpiling For Large Future Paydays

* We Do Not Offer Legal or Accounting Advice. All Services Are The Opinions Based on Our Expertise in The Industry and We Offer No Claims or Responsibility For Future Earnings or Losses

Free To All Paid Mastermind Members
Investment in Yourself - $197

Email our office at erik@TheRealErikStark.com and we will set up a brief call to discuss how to get you from where you are to where you want to be in the shortest time with the least amount of hassle.

Workshops (90 Minutes) Locally In Boca Raton Fl and Ferndale MI

- Live Workshops Taught By Active Real Estate Entrepreneurs
- Classes Forming Monthly For Investors, Realtors and Entrepreneurs
- Topics Include:
1. 1 Simple Way To Increase Your Business With More Focus, Less Overwhelm and Measurable Progress **(Our Most Requested Workshop)**
2. The Secret to Marketing Most Investors Will Never Know And Your Clients Are Begging To Receive **(A True Game Changer When Implemented)**
3. How To Discover Motivated Sellers (Faster), Reveal Their Pain Points (Easier) and Lead Them Down The Path of Profitability Without Conflict, Resistance or Opposition (Automatically)

Investment In Yourself - $97

Annual Mastermind - Are you looking to be a part of a small group of investors that have figured out whats really working? We work with a small group of investors throughout the year. Typically less than 12 at a time simply because we still run a full time business and there is a lot of work that goes into creating content and action plans for those who want to get to the next level. This is not open for new investors. You must be operating a minimum six figure annual business. Register for our next mastermind right here. (www.SelfManagingFreedom.com)

One on One - There is no one size fits all glove that will teach you real estate. **Truth is no coach can help anyone if they don't know where they need the help**. In the medical world, diagnosing without knowing the symptoms is called malpractice.

Work with US (not some assigned coach) to hone your skills, determine target markets, create marketing pieces that stick, learn how to convert sellers, increase property values, understand zoning, how to assign for larger paydays (our smallest assignment in the last 3 years was $25,000, up to $85,000). We can take you from where you are to where you want to go in the shortest time with the least amount of hassle. You must be operating a minimum six figure annual business. Six month commitment (although most stick with us for a few years leaving few openings to join) Apply For One on One Monthly Education Right Here.

Motivation to Keep You Going
Build A Life Free From Vacation

Learn to Love What Others Will Not Tolerate

Never, Never, Never Give Up

"As To Methods, There May Be A Million and Then Some. But Principles Are Few. The Man Who Grasps Principles, Can Select His Own Methods, The Man Who Grasps Methods, Ignoring Principles, Is Sure to Have Trouble" Emerson

Where Others Stop, I Just Get Started

It Doesn't Have To Be Perfect. It Just Has To Be Going

Value Was Meant To Be Costly. If It Doesn't Cost Much, We Wouldn't Appreciate The Value

Do Your Work With Your Whole Heart and You Will Succeed...These Is Such Little Competition

I Went Looking for Something Powerful...and found my notes

Seek Freedom and Be Captive of Your Desires. Seek Discipline and Find Your Liberty

One Last Note From Erik...

I want to sincerely thank you for choosing to invest in yourself. It excites me to see people who are willing to demand more from life and put forth the effort to achieve greatness.

I am also very thankful for our time we spent together and look forward to seeing your growth. As you will see as we get to know each other, we are much more than just real estate guys. Real estate is just the money side to our lives.

We look onward to your coming greatness and hope you keep us included and updated along the way.

Remember, success is not pursued.

Success ensues your massive action.

See you at the top,

Erik Stark
Erik@TheRealErikStark.com
#whatmatters
#menofpurpose

www.ingramcontent.com/pod-product-compliance
Lightning Source LLC
Chambersburg PA
CBHW070319190526
45169CB00005B/1671